Really Short Walks
South Devon

Paul White

Bossiney Books

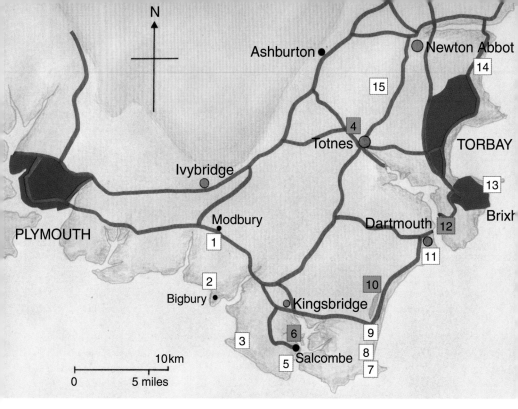

The approximate locations of the walks in this book –
easier walks are indicated by green squares

All the walks in this book were checked prior to printing, at which time
the instructions were correct. However, changes can occur in the
countryside over which neither the author nor the publisher has any
control. Please let us know if you encounter any serious problems.

This reprint 2014
First published 2009 by
Bossiney Books Ltd, 33 Queens Drive, Ilkley LS29 9QW
www.bossineybooks.com
© 2009 Paul White   All rights reserved
ISBN 978-1-906474-07-2

Acknowledgements
The maps are by Graham Hallowell
Cover based on a design by Heards Design Partnership
Photographs by the author
Printed in Great Britain by R Booth Ltd, Penryn, Cornwall

Introduction

The walks in this book are mostly 3-5km (2-3 miles) in length. Some are easy, others short but challenging. All have been chosen to show the wonderful scenery of south Devon – cliffs and beaches, woodland and moorland, as well as very attractive farmland. We have not suggested how long they will take, because readers' walking abilities will vary considerably, nor have we selected the walks with pushchairs or wheelchairs in mind: most would be unsuitable in this often uneven terrain.

Clothing and footwear

Do go prepared. Devon's weather can change rapidly, and even within a short walk there may be a considerable temperature difference when you climb from a sheltered valley to a cliff top exposed to a Channel breeze. Always carry extra layers of clothing as well as a waterproof. On most paths, especially inland, you are likely to come across briars, thorns and nettles, so bare legs are a liability.

There will be some mud at most times of the year and perhaps a lot of mud and puddles in winter and after a wet spell. Ideally, therefore, wear walking boots – and certainly not sandals! Walking any distance in wellington boots is not recommended, as they don't provide ankle support and can apparently be bad for your spine, but a single short walk of under 5km shouldn't cause a problem for most people. Just watch out for uneven ground, especially on the cliff path. I find a walking pole is a considerable help. It is sensible to carry water with you, as dehydration causes tiredness.

Safety

Be careful when walking the cliff path because it is not fenced off from the drop. Go no nearer the edge than you have to: you might be standing on an overhang. Take special care when the path does take you near the edge, and keep a close eye on children and dogs.

The sketch maps in this book are just that – sketches. You may want to carry an OS 1:25,000 map for extra information.

The countryside

Despite many pressures on their livelihoods, farmers are still trying to make a living from the land you will pass through. Please respect their crops. Leave gates closed or open as you find them, and keep dogs under control, especially during the lambing season.

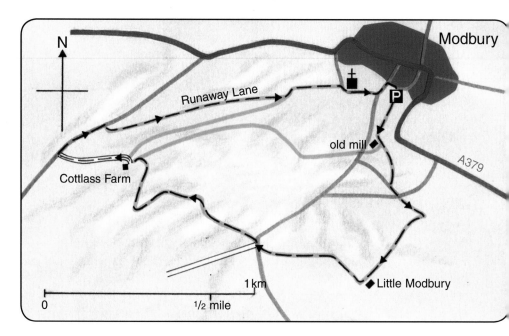

Walk 1   Modbury

Distance: 5.2km (3¹/₄ miles)
Character: An inland walk of great charm, with views over the historic town and towards Dartmoor. Ancient tracks are a feature of the walk, including a holloway which was once a medieval main road – it may be seriously muddy so wear boots. Two moderately steep ascents.

Start from Modbury's Poundwell Meadow car park. Take the public footpath from the far end of the car park. Pass an old mill house and continue ahead across a stile into a meadow. Cross the footbridge over the stream and continue in the same direction to a stile. Turn left up the narrow lane, then cross the lane ahead into a footpath.

After climbing to a stile, the path turns abruptly right. After 50m, watch out for a pair of stiles on the left. Cross these and bear right as waymarked. Cross another pair of stiles and bear left as waymarked. Go through a gate and pass Little Modbury Farm on your left.

Immediately after the next gate turn right (the waymark is easily missed). Keep the hedge on your right, then cut diagonally to a gate in the top left corner. Keep the hedge on your left through one field, then bear slightly right through the next field to a stile.

Turn right down the lane, passing the entrance to Butland then bearing left into an old track. This takes a strangely indirect course,

4

finally reaching Cottlass Farm. Ignore the bridleway and then the footpath on the right, and follow the tarmac track up to a lane.

Turn sharp right. After 230 m, turn right into RUNAWAY LANE. Follow this ancient holloway for just over 1 km, ignoring side turnings. Finally arriving at tarmac, turn right, pass the church, and turn left at a road junction. Keep right at the next junction, back to the car park.

Runaway Lane

A plaque at the Modbury end explains that the lane is so called because a Royalist force retreated along it after the second Battle of Modbury in 1643. As they had fought a force four times larger for many hours, it was less 'running away' than 'strategic retreat', but the battle was a major Parliamentary victory, since the siege of Plymouth was lifted as a result.

What the plaque does not mention is that Runaway Lane was the main road between Dartmouth and Plymouth at that time, and still appears as such in road maps of 1675 and even 1765. The retreating Royalist army numbered 2000, the pursuing Parliamentarians nearly 10,000, with baggage carts and artillery. Just imagine what the lane must have looked like after they had passed – and try not to grumble about the mud today!

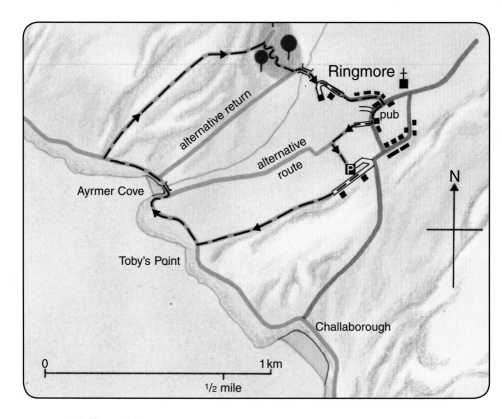

Ayrmer Cove

Ringmore

pub

Toby's Point

Challaborough

N

0   1 km

½ mile

Walk 2   Ringmore

Distance: 3.8km (2¼ miles) or 2.5km (1½ miles)
Character: A walk of great variety, with magnificent coastal views
in both directions, a superb cove with a beach, a short stretch of
delightful woodland and one of south Devon's most attractive villages.
It is, however, quite a strenuous walk, with two steep descents and a
fairly steep ascent. The shorter alternative version has easier gradients,
but is more limited in its scope.

Start from the Ayrmer Cove car park at Ringmore. From the point
where the lane enters the car park, face the village and turn right at a
post with a yellow arrow marked TOBY'S POINT then right again along
the track past 'The Laurels'. The track becomes a footpath, with views
of Burgh Island to the left.

On reaching the coast path at Toby's Point, turn right. The path
descends steeply. At the foot, turn left across the footbridge and follow
the path steeply upwards. Near the top of the cliff, turn right. (This is
a permissive path, not a full right-of-way.)

A prolonged but gentle climb leads to the summit, where the path changes direction. Keep the hedge on your right. Go through a kissing gate into the wood. When the path divides, turn sharp right. The path winds and zig-zags down. At the foot, a gate leads to a path junction*.

Turn left, RINGMORE, and follow the path round to the right. Keep left at a track, and then to the left of Lower Manor Farm and continue up the lane into the village. At a lane junction, turn right to pass the Journey's End pub (or not, as the case may be) and then bear left uphill.

At the next junction turn right past 'Smugglers Cottage'. When the tarmac ends, bear left on PUBLIC BRIDLEWAY. A gate leads into National Trust land. Turn left here, back to the car park.

A shorter alternative

Take the pedestrian exit from the car park, beside the information board. After 50m, turn left and follow the path down to Ayrmer Cove. Cross the footbridge and immediately turn right. This path joins the main route at the point marked * in the text above.

7

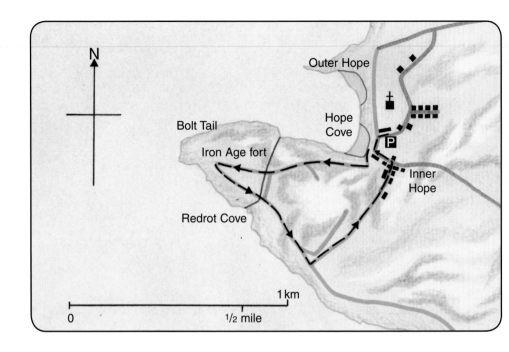

Walk 3   Hope Cove

Distance: 2.7km (1³/4 miles) from Inner Hope. It is also possible to start from Outer Hope, adding about 800m (¹/2 mile) in total.

Character: A steady climb to an Iron Age promontory fort, with breathtaking views in both directions along the coast, then an attractive valley leads to the delightful cottages of Inner Hope.

From the Inner Hope Layby Long Stay car park, walk down to the beach. Cross behind the beach, then take the steps beside the lifeboat house (COAST PATH SALCOMBE). The path leads through a small area of woodland, then up to the entrance of the Bolt Tail promontory fort.

Enter the fort and climb to the highest point to enjoy the views, then turn and follow the path with the sea on your right.

Follow the coast path as far as a junction, just before a gate. Turn left, inland, HOPE COVE, and keep the hedge on your right. Follow the path to the bottom of the field, then into trees. Ignore side turns and you will arrive at a gate.

Follow the lane down to a T-junction, then turn left back to the lifeboat station and retrace your steps.

The beach at Inner Hope in the foreground, with Outer Hope beyond

Part of an extensive view from Bolt Tail of all the beaches from Bantham to Hope

Cottages at Inner Hope

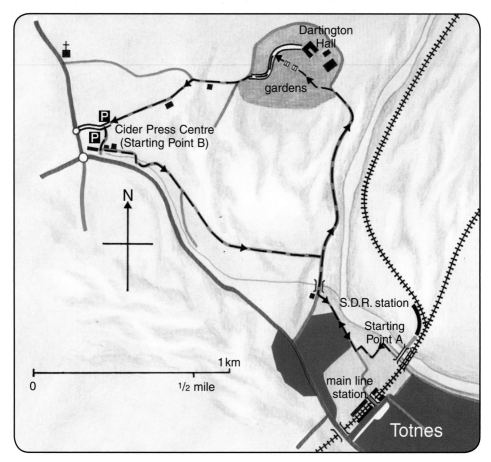

Walk 4   Dartington

Distance: 3.6km (2¹/₄ miles) for the basic circuit. 5.6km (3¹/₂ miles) from either the South Devon Railway or the mainline station. A little more from Totnes itself.

Character: In essence a circuit from the Cider Press Centre, with its refreshments and interesting craft shops, to Dartington Hall and back, but it can be started from Totnes or from the steam railway or main line stations. Pleasant riverside, and a lovely garden to explore at Dartington Hall. (A donation of £2 per person is requested to visit the gardens: walking groups must obtain permission in advance. No dogs. Alternatively, use the lane around the north of the house.)

From the South Devon Railway station, leave by the path to the town, cross the river and turn right on the RIVERSIDE WALK at what we call 'Starting Point A'.

10

From the main line station, Platform 1 side, turn left through a car park, signed for RIVERSIDE WALK and for SOUTH DEVON RAILWAY. Follow the path to the river and turn left on the Riverside Walk. Cross under the railway to our Starting Point A.

From Starting Point A, the path changes direction several times before crossing a stream. Turn right on Cycle Path 2. On reaching a road, turn right past the gates and lodge and follow the road. Ignore the cycle path to the left.

* Continue to follow the road uphill. When it makes a sharp turn to the right, keep left, through a gate, into Dartington Gardens. You may well want to explore, but the simple route is to continue uphill, then to take the flights of steps which lead on in the same direction. When you arrive at a tarmac driveway turn left, and follow it as it winds up to a gate into a lane. Turn left along the footway parallel to the lane.

Pass High Cross House, then fork left, PUBLIC FOOTPATH, and shortly continue ahead SHOPS DARTINGTON.

'Starting Point B' is the upper car park of the Cider Press Centre. Walk down to the lowest level of the Centre, and turn left, towards Totnes, on a cycle path beside the river. At a fork, bear left on the cycle path. When you reach a road, turn left if you are doing the basic circuit and continue from the * in the text above.

Or turn right for Totnes and retrace your steps.

11

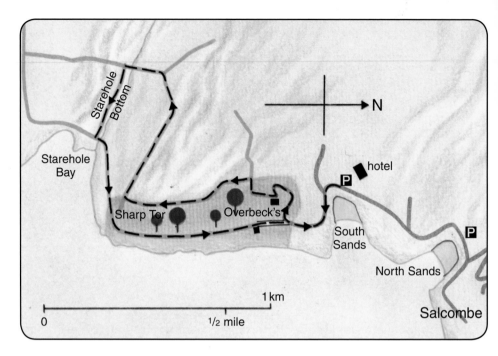

Walk 5 Overbeck's and Sharp Tor

Distance: 4.4km (2³/4 miles) from South Sands
Character: One of the most attractive and dramatic sections of the
south Devon coast, walking out at a high level and returning at a
lower level. Quite strenuous in places.

Start from the Tide's Reach car park at South Sands. (Alternatively
there is limited on-road parking further on, but please leave the
parking at and near Overbeck's for visitors to the house and its lovely
garden – unless of course you want to combine the walk with a visit.)
The walk took me 70 minutes, which may help you decide how much
parking to pay for.

From the car park, turn right and follow the lane up towards
Overbeck's. Fork right for OVERBECKS and climb the lane, which
swings left and past the small car park. Just before the main gates
of the house, turn right on a footpath. The path climbs past the
Overbeck's gardens and into a wood.

Turn left, SHARP TOR STAREHOLE BOLT HEAD. At Sharp Tor, where
the path swings right, do walk a few metres out to see the wonderful
view back towards Salcombe. Then continue on the path along the
crest. Follow it round to the left and down to cross the stream in the

12

valley – which is called Starehole Bottom – then turn left downhill, parallel to the stream till you meet the Coast Path.

Turn left, OVERBECKS TOR WOODS SALCOMBE and take the dramatic Courtenay Path, said to have been cut for the benefit of visitors by Viscount Courtenay in the 1860s. When you reach the lane, keep right and retrace your footsteps to South Sands.

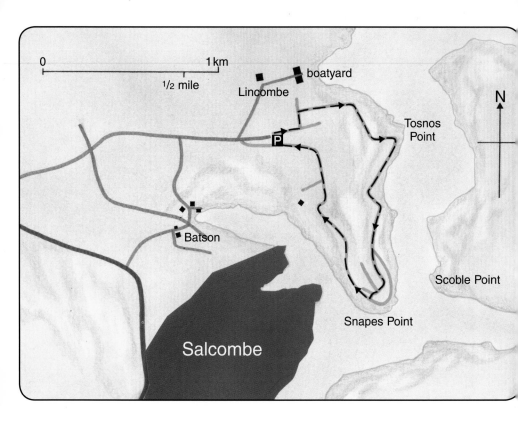

Walk 6   Snapes Point

Distance: 3.3km (2 miles)
Character: A sequence of glorious views over Salcombe harbour and the Kingsbridge estuary. There are no steep hills, and the hardest part is finding the car park from which you start!

To get there: From Malborough, take the A381 towards SALCOMBE, *then take the second turning on the left, a narrow lane signed* HORSCOMBE LINCOMBE. *Follow* LINCOMBE *at the next two junctions, then bear right at the third junction into the National Trust car park.*

From the car park, take the footpath signed LINCOMBE SNAPE POINT. After 200 m, turn left through an unsigned pedestrian gate. The official footpath now keeps the hedge on the left round three sides of the field, with views over the boatyard and up-river.

Ignore temptations to leave the field, traverse three sides then leave by a gate. Follow the path which turns immediately left towards the water, and (again) keep the hedge on your left around the bottom edge

14

of this field. Go through a gate at the end and continue (with the hedge on your left!) to a fork in the path.

Bear right, gently uphill, and continue ahead at a wooden waymark post for a spectacular view of rivers and creeks, and then a view over Salcombe itself. Keep left at a bench, to leave the field by a gate. Descend steps and turn right along a broad path. Continue ahead at a path junction and climb gently to arrive back at the car park.

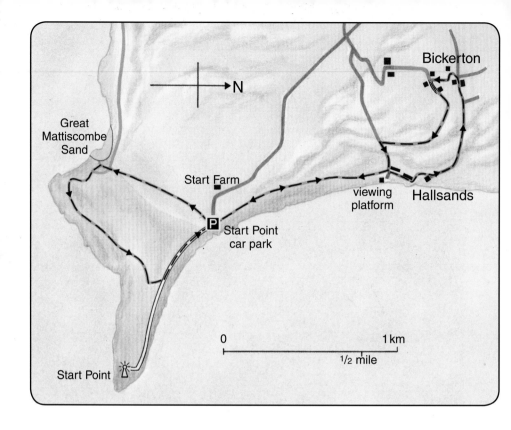

Walks 7 and 8   From Start Point car park

To Mattiscombe and the lighthouse

Distance: 2.4km (1 1/2 miles) or 3.4km (2 miles)
Character: Short but quite strenuous. A lovely beach, and a dramatic section of coast path – very near the edge in places, so take care if you have children or dogs – and then a glorious view from the spiky ridge of Start Point. An optional extra 500m each way will take you to the lighthouse.

Start from the Start Point car park (SX 821375). Leave by a gate at the bottom left corner and turn right down a path.

Descend a valley to Great Mattiscombe Sand, and a junction with the coast path. Continue ahead, START POINT.

After turning sharp left, the path winds along the cliff, sometimes very close to the edge, then climbs to the ridge of Start Point, where an impressive view suddenly opens up. For the lighthouse, turn right down the access drive. Otherwise turn left, back up to the car park.

To Hallsands

Distance: 4km (2¹/₂ miles)
Character: Mostly coast path, with a short inland diversion. The old fishing village of Hallsands was destroyed by the sea – but as a direct result of Government activity. Dredging offshore in the 1890s for sand and gravel to expand the Plymouth naval dockyard destabilised the beach and storms did the rest. By 1917 only one house remained habitable. The Government took seven years to pay compensation.

Leave the Start Point car park northward by the Coast Path, with the sea to your right. Follow it down to Hallsands. When you reach houses, divert right to the viewing platform from which you can see the little that remains of the original village.

Continue on the coast path to a beach car park and take the lane which leads inland to the hamlet of Bickerton. Turn left (signed as a dead end) down to Bickerton Farm, and follow the tarmac track as it winds left then right. When you reach a glass-fronted cottage turn left. An enclosed track leads to a field.

Keep the bottom fence of the field on your left. Continue to a stile in the far left corner. Turn left along the lane, which will bring you to the Coast Path. Turn right. The path leads gently upwards, back to the car park.

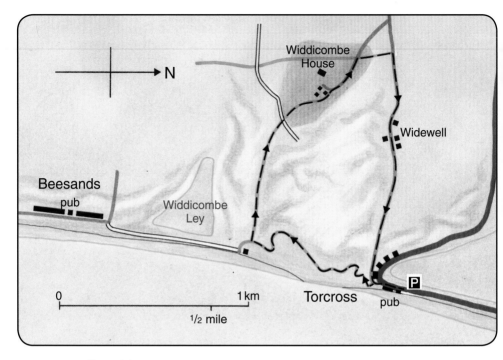

Walk 9 Torcross

Distance: 4.1 km (2½ miles)
Character: A long haul up to the top of the hill above Torcross is fully compensated by magnificent views over Slapton Ley and Beesands. The inland section is through attractive fields, woodland and parkland, then back along a very quiet lane.

Park at Torcross, either in the Torcross lay-by or in the car park by the Sherman tank. (You could alternatively start from Beesands, see map.) Walk to the centre of Torcross and, where the main road turns right, continue ahead up a lane, signed UNSUITABLE FOR HEAVY GOODS VEHICLES.

After 50 m, turn left, PUBLIC FOOTPATH, up steps. At the top, divert left a few metres for a view over Slapton Sands and Slapton Ley, then retrace your steps and take the access drive. Turn left on a tarmac drive at the acorn sign and immediately bear right at another acorn sign.

The path winds upwards, crosses a field and enters woodland. It circles a disused quarry, which is out of sight, then descends to a path junction. You might wish to continue down to Beesands, where there is a pub and a beach. Otherwise, turn right, PUBLIC FOOTPATH.

18

Keep the hedge on your left for the full length of the field, then bear right as signed to a stile. Cross a track and another stile takes you into woodland. Follow the well defined path, then a track, then a driveway through parkland. At a path junction, turn right, PUBLIC FOOTPATH WIDEWELL.

Descend the field to a kissing gate, and turn right along the lane which leads through Widewell. You will want to stop at the Torcross Viewpoint, which doubles as a butterfly sanctuary, before descending to Torcross.

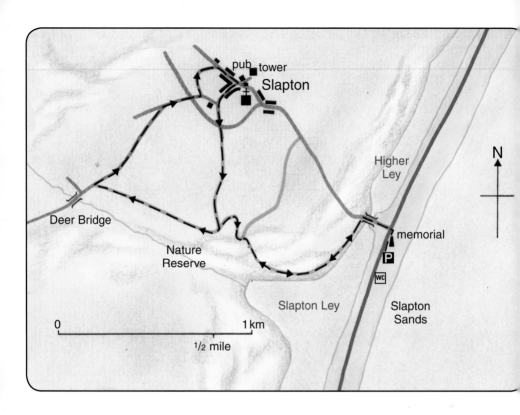

Walk 10   Slapton Ley and Slapton village

Distance: 5km (3¹/₄ miles)
Character: Partly in the Slapton Ley National Nature Reserve, so take your binoculars for bird watching. The path runs beside the freshwater lake, then through marshy woodland. The village of Slapton is both attractive and interesting, dominated by the ruined tower of a medieval collegiate chantry – below which nestles the Tower Inn.

Start from the Memorial Car Park on the shingle beach (SX 829442). Facing inland, turn right along the verge past the memorial obelisk – a thank you from the USA to the local inhabitants, who 'generously left their homes and their lands to provide a battle practice area' in preparation for D-Day.

The Sherman tank at the Torcross end of the shingle beach is a memorial to nearly a thousand American troops who lost their lives in a disastrous exercise, when German e-boats made a surprise attack.

Just beyond the obelisk, cross the main road and take the road towards SLAPTON, crossing the bridge between the Higher and Lower

Leys, then turn left PUBLIC FOOTPATH. The shady path follows the edge of the lake for some way.

At a junction, turn left PUBLIC FOOTPATH and follow a boardwalk. At the next junction, keep left, PUBLIC FOOTPATH DEER BRIDGE. When the path ends, turn sharp right up a lane and climb towards Slapton village.

Continue ahead at GREENBANK, then again at a cross roads. At the next junction, when the road ahead narrows, turn left and follow a lane around the head of the valley. At a T-junction, by 'Crossbow Cottage' and 'Whitebeam', turn right downhill. At 'The Round House', a left turn leads to the Tower Inn and the medieval tower, whilst the right turn leads to the church.

Now retrace your steps for about 50m, and bear left at BROOK STREET CROSS.

Bear left uphill at Stoutts Farmhouse. At a crossroads, continue ahead, PUBLIC FOOTPATH SLAPTON LEY.

At the foot of the hill, turn left, signed PUBLIC FOOTPATH, and retrace your steps along the boardwalk and the lakeside path.

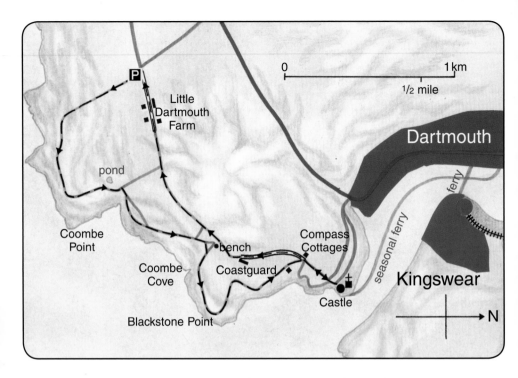

Walk 11 Little Dartmouth to Dartmouth Castle

Distance: 5.3km (3 1/4 miles)
Character: A very attractive stretch of coastal path leading to
Dartmouth's 14th century castle, built to defend what was then one of
England's major ports, and one of the first fortifications to be
purpose-built for artillery. The return involves a long steady climb.

I started from the National Trust car park at Little Dartmouth, but it
is equally possible to start from the Castle, where there is some on-road
parking, or it can be reached by the seasonal ferry from Dartmouth.

From Little Dartmouth Farm car park, take LINK TO COAST PATH
DARTMOUTH CASTLE 2 1/2 MILES. Don't panic – it's actually rather less
than that! Follow the well-beaten path for 500 m to a kissing gate, then
to the left along the coast. Turn left through a gate (Coast Path acorn
sign).

Cross a culvert leading from a pond and after a further 75 m at a
path junction keep right on the Coast Path. Shortly after this the path
divides: for the official path keep next to the bottom edge of the field.
The paths soon rejoin.

22

Go through a gate and keep right (yellow sign). The path descends, at first gently, then turns right down a steep coombe towards the sea. Keep left when the path divides. A gate leads into scrubland. At the next junction, the dead-end path to the right leads to a viewpoint.

From here the path begins to climb quite steeply through trees and around a cove. It becomes an access drive. On reaching cottages ahead of you, turn right down the lane. The Coast Path immediately diverges to the right: it is very pretty but quite hard going, with steps. The lane is a much easier option!

When you reach a parking area, turn right COAST PATH DARTMOUTH CASTLE.

For the return, from the Castle take COAST PATH STOKE FLEMING. Climb to a lane and turn left, taking the tarmac track uphill, ACCESS TO COMPASS COTTAGES AND COASTGUARD STATION. At the cottages keep right, BRIDLEWAY LITTLE DARTMOUTH and climb to and past the Coastguard Station.

The tarmac ends here, but the old track continues, around the head of the coombe and to a gate. From the gate the enclosed track leads to Little Dartmouth Farm. Go through the farm complex and you will arrive at the car park.

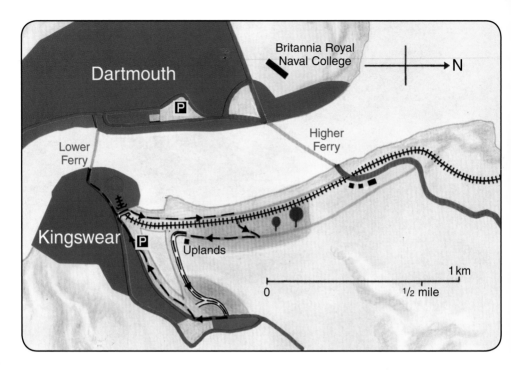

Walk 12 Kingswear

Distance: 3.5km (2¼ miles)
Character: Starting from the Lower Ferry at Kingswear, or from the railway station, this walk gives great views of steam trains, yachts (and sometimes larger vessels), historic Dartmouth and the Dart estuary, as well as some very attractive woodland.

From the landing ramp at the Lower Ferry, turn left and follow the footway of the main road uphill past the station. Turn left onto an iron footbridge across the railway.

On the far side, a well marked path leads through the marina and boatyard and across the creek, before adopting a route between the water's edge and the railway track.

About half-way between the two ferries, turn right on a footpath which crosses the track and enters Hoodown woods. Climb steadily to a path junction, and turn sharp right. This path leads through woodland, and emerges onto an access drive at 'Uplands'.

The drive soon swings left. Follow it, ignoring side turnings, till it emerges on the main road, which is one-way, uphill, at this point and only intermittently busy when traffic leaves the ferry.

Turn right down the road. Soon there is a pavement/footway, then on the right a signed footpath. This runs parallel to the road until you reach the marina car park. Climb the steps to the road and continue in the same direction towards the iron footbridge, then retrace your steps to the ferry.

An alternative route via Dartmouth

Distance: 2.75 km (1³/4 miles)
As can be seen from the sketch map, an excellent alternative – a virtually flat stroll – is to continue along the path beside the railway to the Higher Ferry, cross to Dartmouth and follow the promenade as far as you can, then turn right, left and left again back to the Lower Ferry.

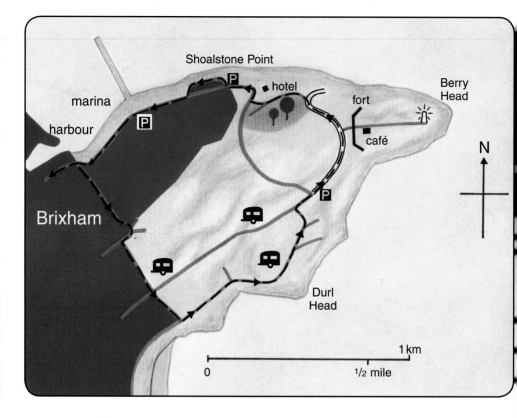

Walk 13   Berry Head and Brixham

Distance: 4.5 km (2³/₄ miles)

Character: Two attractive and very different stretches of coast path, either side of Berry Head, connected by walking through part of Brixham – that section of the walk is on road, but all the streets have pavements. One long climb from the harbour, otherwise easy walking.

You could use the walk to explore the Brixham harbour area, or you could start from Brixham and walk out.

Take the broad tarmac track from the far end of the car park at Berry Head. Pass the fort, built in 1795 to protect an existing battery from landward attack. (A stroll down to Britain's smallest lighthouse and back will add 1 km to the walk.)

Continue ahead, HARDY'S HEAD BATTERY. Cross a cattle grid. Ignore the first path left. After only 50 m continue ahead on the COAST PATH. Fork right at the next COAST PATH sign.

26

On reaching a lane, turn right, passing the Berry Head Hotel. At the Shoalstone car park, turn right through the car park and follow the Coast Path past a swimming pool. On rejoining the street, turn right. Follow it, with good views over the marina and breakwater, as far as Ranscombe Road, and then 100m further to a bench with an iconic view over the harbour.

Unless you want to continue into the town, retrace your steps and bear right up Ranscombe Road, PAIGNTON KINGSWEAR. Keep right at the top into Higher Ranscombe Road, then turn left into Centry Road. Pass the no entry signs. Cross Gillard Road and take the footpath opposite.

At the end, turn left – unsigned, but it is the Coast Path. Follow the Coast Path past various junctions. At a notice board marking the entry to the Berry Head Country Park, a National Nature Reserve, bear left, and left again at the next junction. This will lead you out to a lane. Turn right to return to the car park.

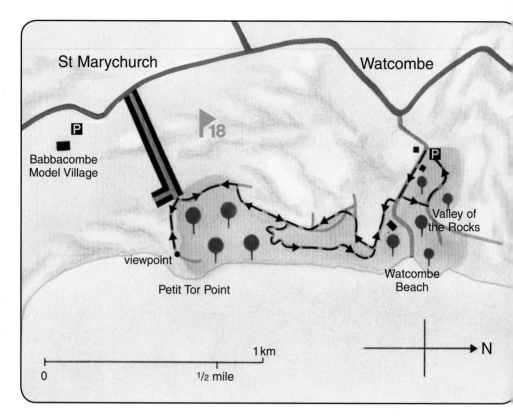

Walk 14 Watcombe

Distance: 4.75 km (3 miles) but can be shortened
Character: Quite a strenuous walk, mostly in deciduous woodland,
with occasional views of the sea – more in winter than in summer!

I started from the Watcombe car park (SX 922674) but you could start
from St Marychurch. From the Watcombe car park, turn left down
the lane towards the beach. After 200 m turn right, COAST PATH TO
BABBACOMBE and climb the steps.

At a fork, bear right (i.e. not the Coast Path). Keep left at the next
junction and cross the head of the coombe, then keep right, uphill.
Continue ahead at the next two junctions, rejoining the Coast Path.

Follow the Coast Path till it turns inland up a street (Petitor Road).
You could head inland to visit St Marychurch, or the Babbacombe
Model Village.

Otherwise, turn left here into an attractive semi-wild area. Follow
the well-beaten path down as far as a bench with a lovely view over

28

Babbacombe. Retrace your steps, rejoining the Coast Path. Pass the golf course and turn right, COAST PATH WATCOMBE. After a welcome flat stretch, turn sharp right, COAST PATH and follow the coast path signs. Turn left when you reach the beach access lane.

Almost immediately, turn right, COAST PATH MAIDENCOMBE. At a path junction in the Valley of the Rocks (which owes much of its distinctive scenery to former quarrying) turn left up the John Musgrave Heritage Trail. The path climbs gently along the side of the valley, before abruptly entering the car park.

Further walks in Torbay

Another Bossiney Walks Book, *Shortish Walks: Torbay and Dartmouth*, includes several walks which are either under 5km, or can easily be shortened to that length. These include:

Meadfoot, Kent's Cavern and Ansteys Cove
A Torquay history walk
Cockington from Torre Abbey Sands
Churston Ferrers
Scabbacombe Sands
Coleton Fishacre

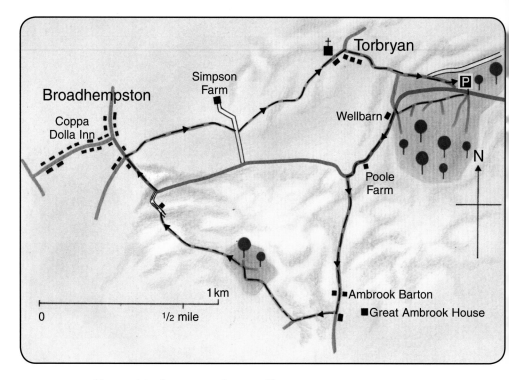

Walk 15   Torbryan and Broadhempston

Distance: 6.5 km (4 miles) though this can be reduced a little if you can find somewhere to park considerately in Torbryan. See the sketch map for the route modification needed.

Character: Woodland on Orley Common, but most of the walk is farmland, with extensive views over fields of red earth and green crops. Two interesting villages, each with a pub and a church.

Start from the car park on Orley Common (SX 827666). To get there, from the A381 Newton Abbot-Totnes road turn into Ipplepen, then take the Broadhempston Road. The car park is somewhat hidden, on the right.

Cross the lane and go through the gate onto the common. Turn right on a path parallel to the lane.

There are many, many paths and the trick is to stay close to and parallel to the lane. I took a left fork, then crossed another track at right angles, then kept right at several junctions. The path descended steeply, then a gate on the right led back to the lane. Turn left along the lane.

You should arrive at Wellbarn Cross! Follow BROADHEMPSTON: this lane can be quite busy at times, so take care. At the next junction, turn left LITTLEHEMPSTON TOTNES which is quieter.

About 100 m beyond Ambrook Barton, turn right on a PUBLIC FOOTPATH. This is waymarked across several fields. Turn right at a path junction and follow the waymarks into a young wood. At a path crossing, turn left, PUBLIC FOOTPATH. Ultimately a farm track brings you down to a lane: turn left into BROADHEMPSTON.

Opposite the turning to Staverton, turn right onto a footpath. (To explore the village, and perhaps visit the Coppa Dolla Inn, continue along the lane and take the first left, then retrace your steps.) The footpath is well waymarked through fields.

Cross a farm access track and continue across more fields to Torbryan. Pass the Old Church House Inn, and the white painted church, then turn right (IPPLEPEN) at a T-junction.

At Broadway Cross, turn left, IPPLEPEN, then bear right at a fork, quite steeply uphill. Just 15 m before the junction at ORLEY COMMON, turn left up a narrow woodland path. Keep taking the right-hand path and you'll arrive back at the car park.

Some other Bossiney walks books

Really Short Walks South Dartmoor
Shortish Walks on Dartmoor
Shortish Walks in East Devon
Shortish Walks near Exeter
Shortish Walks – The South Devon Coast
Shortish Walks – Torbay and Dartmouth

Some Bossiney 'Shortish Guides'

Dartmouth
Exeter
Plymouth
The South Hams

Some other Bossiney books about Devon

Devon Beach and Cove Guide
Devon's Castles
Devon Smugglers – the truth behind the fiction
Devon's Geology
Devon's History
Devon's Railway Heritage
Torbay – the Visible History
Traditional Devon Recipes